PRAISE &
Encouragement

PRAISE &

Encouragement

By
SANDRA M. RILEY

ARPress
ILLUMINATING IDEAS
EMPOWERING VOICES

ARPress
45 Dan Road Suite 36
Canton MA 02021

Hotline: 1(888) 821-0229
Fax: 1(508) 545-7580

Ordering Information:
Quantity Sales. Special discounts are available on quantity purchases by corporations, associations, and others. For details, contact the publisher at the address above.

Printed in the United States of America.

ISBN-13   Paperback   979-8-89330-908-9
               eBook   979-8-89330-910-2
               Hardback   979-8-89330-909-6

Library of Congress Control Number: 2024903337

Dedicated
To
My Family
My Pastor
My Church Family
&
All God's Children…
God Loves You!

Table Of Contents

Introduction xi

PART 1: Praise Ye the Lord Psalm 150:6 1
God's Love 2
Jesus 3
Holy Ghost 4
Excellent 5
Praise 6
Joy 7
Omnipotent 8
I Am Grateful 9
God's Gift 10
He Is 11
The Powerful Name 12
Give Thanks 13
You Are Everything 14
A Love Like No Other 15
He Knocks 16
Lord, I Owe It All to You! 17
Lord, You Have Been Good To Me! 18
God's Amazing Grace 19
My Best Friend 20
The Wonderful One 21
Thank You, Lord! 22
He Is Worthy 23
Father In Heaven 24

PART 2: Encouragement for Your Soul 25
Wait On The Lord 26
Use Me, Lord 27
Supreme 28
Promises 29
The Christian Way 30
To Be Christlike 31

Hang In There 32
Faith 33
Do Not Give In 34
Dear Lord 35
Prayer 36
Who Loves You? 37
The Brighter Side 38
Watching Over Me 39
The Burden-Bearer 40
Believe! 41
Ordinary People 42
I Am Satisfied 43
What You Can Bear 44
He Is There 45
To The Sky 46
Brand-New Life 47
Forgive Us 48
You Are Never Alone 49
Gentleness 50
The Road 51
Your Heart's Desire 52
What You Need 53
Be Content 54
In Times Of Trouble 55
To Be A Star 56
Give It Up 57
Call On Him 58
Trouble Don't Last Always 59
The Precious Blood 60
What I Can Do 61
Your Touch 62
He Speaks 63
Which Way Do You Walk? 64
Shine On Me 65
Keep Your Eyes On Him 66
God's Chosen One 67
You Cannot Hide 68

Heaven Smiles 69
Try Him 70
God's Unchanging Hand 71
Lord, My Desire Is To Be Closer to you! 72
He Open Doors.. 73
Shower Of Blessings... 74
Assured Acceptance.. 75
Do You Know Jesus? 76
I Need You, Lord 77
Talk To God 78
He Lifted Me 79
He Saved Me 80
No Turning Back 81
Rest In You.. 82
No Room For Defeat.. 83
Jesus Supplies All My Needs 84
Everything Is Alright.. 85
I Must Go On 86
You Had Mercy On Me 87
Victory 88
The Master's Plan.. 89
Because You Will Not Let Me Go 90
Only For A While... 91
Trust In God.. 92
Jesus Makes Me Glad.. 93
Faith Is The Only Way 94
Try Jesus 95
I Can't Turn Around 96
He Carries You Through 97
Long-Suffering... 98
Help Is On The Way... 99
The Rock 100
Strength... 101
Heaven-Bound 102
Here Is Something For Everyone........................... 103
About The Author 104

Introduction

I give Glory, Honor, and Praise to God the Father, Jesus Christ the Son, and to the Precious Holy Ghost. I count it a blessing and a privilege to be used by God in a special way. What I mean is through the Power of the Holy Ghost, God has allowed His expression of Love to come forth through the Art of Poetry. James 1:17 states, "Every good gift and every perfect gift is from above, and cometh down from the Father of lights, with whom is no variableness, neither shadow of turning." God's gift to His people is His Love through poetry. God expresses himself to us in different ways. We can praise Him because He is a Mighty God. To me, God is El Shaddai, "One who is Self-Sufficient." Also, we can think about His goodness, His mercy, and His grace. All of these and even more are expressed through poetry. Everyone has a "valley experience." When I say "valley experience," I am referring to trials, tribulations, and persecutions we go through in our lives. But through it all, God is in the midst. He loves us, He is taking care of us, and He will see us through the storms in our lives.

Encouragement is being inspired and finding hope to know we can go on. Yes, we can go on in Jesus' Name.

I would like to introduce Praise & Encouragement, a book of poetry that praises God for all the things He has done and gives encouragement for those who are going through something. Be encouraged in knowing that God is always with you. Just look to Jesus Christ our Lord and Savior. He will see you through. When you read Praise & Encouragement, ask the Holy Ghost to open your mind to receive the blessings God has in store for you. God loves you. Let Him express His love through the Art of Poetry in Praise & Encouragement. Allow the Holy Ghost to minister to your soul, regulate your mind, renew your spirit, and set you free. May God bless you richly as you read Praise & Encouragement page by page. I believe everyone who reads this book will find something in it that is appropriate for them. Praise God and be encouraged, my brothers and sisters.

In Jesus Christ,

Sandra M. Riley, Author of
Praise & Encouragement

PART 1:
Praise Ye the Lord
Psalm 150:6

God's Love

God's Love has been so good to me
He cares, I really know
As far as I can plainly see
He always takes the show.
God's Love has been so good to me

When I feel down and out
I know that there will truly be
A way He will make me shout.

God's Love has been so good to me
I will work to serve Him well
For I can feel the glory that will be
Of all that He will tell.

Jesus

Jesus in the world is a bright shining light
One that glows both day and night
A shine that is bright with all its might
Which lets us know that things are right.

Jesus took on our sins and died
Because we are loved through and through
We will be tested and tried
And with Him we become creatures
who are new.

Jesus will come again someday
When He returns I want to be ready
Leading up to that time along the way
In Jesus my life will be steady.

Holy Ghost

We need God, Jesus, and the Holy Ghost too
As the THREE-IN-ONE work together
The Threesome will always see you through
No matter what kind of weather.

The Holy Ghost dwells in us
When we give up our lives
He listens to us make a fuss
But it is He who helps us to strive.

The Holy Ghost will dwell in those
Who want Him to
So why not allow Him to work in you?
He is your comforter, teacher, and guide too
So allow the Holy Ghost to do what He
needs to do.

Excellent

Who is Excellent, Awesome, and Great?
He cares about how you rate
He knows when you need to wait
He is always on time, never late.

The One who loves you above all others.
Who is more than a mother or a brother
One who does not attempt to smother
Because He freely wants our love, one
from another.

Who is Excellent, Awesome, and Great?
With Him you can highly rate
So be strong in Him and wait
God is Excellent, Awesome, and Great!

Praise

We need to praise Him all in all
During winter, spring, summer, and fall
There is no situation too large or small
God is the One we are to call.

God deserves all of our praise
For what He has truly done
Since His own Son He did raise
God's praises should be second to none.

Praise Him, Praise Him all day long
Praise Him at night with a glorious song
Praise Him when you are depressed and sad
For His Love will make you glad.

Joy

Joy is what keeps me going
It is what I feel in knowing
Joy is great, wonderful, and showing
That God's love has me glowing.

Joy is something that needs to be spread
For Joy is nothing if only read
So have Joy in your life today
Because the Lord will make a way.

Joy will always keep me going
Joy will always keep me knowing
That what I am really showing
By the grace of God, I am growing.

Omnipotent

What does one mean by Omnipotent?
He is One who is Almighty and Strong
One who was surely sent
To bring our Christian life along.

He helps you to learn
When you have problems you can turn
To Him and begin to earn
What you should so you will not burn.

Who is the Omnipotent One?
He gave His only begotten Son
The Omnipotent One is unconditional love
He is God Almighty in Heaven above.

I Am Grateful

I am grateful for all You have done
I am grateful now I see the sun
I am grateful, now I can run
I am grateful, your chosen one.

Lord, You love me the most
Because You sent the Holy Ghost
I am grateful for this chance
To turn my life around and advance.

I am grateful because of You
I am grateful for all that You do
I am grateful through and through
I am grateful. Lord, I love You!

God's Gift

What can you say about God's Gift?
It can pull you up and give you a lift
It can fill your heart with so much love
That comes from nowhere but above.

Precious is the Gift that is given
To the one who is determined and driven
To seek the Lord without strife
Because He is the One who saved your life.

Yes, God's Gift is what you heard
His Gift is The Powerful Word
God's Gift is also The Mighty Sword
God's Gift is Jesus Christ our Lord!

He Is

He is the sunshine and the light
He is the morning, noon, and night
He is all the Power and the Might
He is the One who knows what is right.

He is what you want and need
He is who brings you through your deeds
He is the One who had to bleed
He is the Bread of Life and He feeds.

He is what you are looking for
He is knocking at your door
He is the beginning, the end, and the core
He is Jesus Christ forevermore!

The Powerful Name

Something wonderful happens to you
And things will never be the same
For there is One who turns the gray skies blue
It is all in the Powerful Name!

All you need to do is call on Him
When the path is gloomy and dim
What is great is you come as you are
Whether you are traveling near or far.

So, you need not feel embarrassed or ashamed.
Because with Him you have Glorious Fame
And His blessings you want to claim
For Jesus Christ is the Powerful Name!

Give Thanks

We need to give thanks for being here
And for God's guidance and direction
If we are not thankful and tend to fear
Our lives will need much correction.

Thank Him when things are well
Thank Him when things are not swell.
Thank Him anyway as you can tell
He picked you up when you fell.

Give thanks because He loves you
Give thanks; at the beginning of time He knew
You were called with a purpose that is true
To do the will of God through and through.

You Are Everything

I need to say You are everything
You are better than a diamond ring
Much joy and happiness You bring
To those who praise You and care to sing.

When I was lost You found me
And I was down and out
You made me glad to look and see
That I could yell and shout.

So if you are looking for a fling
Not a scratch or a string
You do not have to wait until spring
For my God, You Are Everything!

A Love Like No Other

I know a Love like no other
That will keep you in times of trouble
It is passed from one to another
Because it is extra double.

It will make you feel good inside
And give you that extra strength
While you are on your Christian ride
You can run the greatest length.

Who is more than a sister or brother?
Even greater than a father or mother?
One who loves all, one from another
God Almighty is A Love like no other.

He Knocks

He is the One who knocks at the door
Open it, what are you waiting for?
You will not get this chance anymore
When it is too late you will be on the floor.

Jesus is coming; yes, He will return
Get your house in order and start to learn
He is coming back one day
So humble yourselves, seek Him, and pray.

Open the door if it is locked
Become a part of His glorious flock
You already know He is the Rock
So let Jesus Christ in when He knocks.

Lord, I Owe It All to You!

Lord, You brought me a mighty long way
That is why I have to say
When I think of You carrying me through
Lord, I owe it all to You!

You saved me from this awful place
Of danger I almost faced
Because You take the time You do
Lord, I owe it all to You!

You can turn my gray skies blue
You saved me because You love me too
Now my life is all brand new
Lord, I owe it all to You!

Lord, You Have Been Good To Me!

Lord, from what I can see
You fought for me to every degree
So now I see and must agree
Lord, You have been good to me!

You forgave my faults and saw my needs
That is why You planted the seed
For my life to reflect what it is to be
Lord, You have been good to me.

Now Satan is the one who will flee
For You fight my battles and You hold the key
My heart is filled with so much glee
Lord, You have been good to me!

God's Amazing Grace

When we run this human race
We have a great deal to face
Sometimes we are in the wrong place
But what saves us is God's Amazing Grace.

We all have been known to fall short
To the point where we are all out of sorts
But what keeps us in step and in pace
Is God's Amazing Grace.

We do not deserve this pleasure
To be among the righteous treasure
But He forgives us and gives us space
Because this is God's Amazing Grace.

My Best Friend

He hears me when I call on Him
He is there through thick and thin
When life seems gloomy and very dim
He makes sure with Him I will win.

He is with me when I feel I am all alone
He is with me when I need Him most
When I pray and even moan
My Comforter is with me, the Holy Ghost.

In His flock I can blend
Into His form without the worldly trend
He loves me and I will always depend
On Jesus Christ, my Best Friend!

The Wonderful One

He is everything to me
As plain as my eyes can see
His will is really meant to be
On my life since He set me free.

He is my all and all
I look to Him and shall not fall
There is no problem too large or small
All I need to do is call.

He is Glorious, He is Love
He is God's only begotten Son
He is so peaceful like a dove
He is Jesus Christ, The Wonderful One!

Thank You, Lord!

I may not seem like I appreciate You
For all that You have brought me through
Your love is such a great reward
I want to say, "Thank You, Lord!"

I cannot praise You quite enough
For You are with me when times seem tough
When I think I am on sinking sand
You let me know that I can stand.

I will not go through my life without You
Because You are my Shield and my Sword
For the wonderful, glorious things You do
I have to say, "Thank You, Lord!"

He Is Worthy

God is worthy to be praised
For all that He has done
He sent One who died and was raised
His only begotten Son.

God loves you and wants you to live right
Seek Him diligently with all your might
You see before your very sight
Jesus is the Wonderful, Glorious Light.

God is the Greatest, He is for you
So turn to Him and begin to feel new
He set the task for what you are to do
He is worthy and He is oh so true.

Father In Heaven

Father in Heaven, we look to Thee
For all that we need from You
We grow to learn that our eyes can see
That God, You know what to do.

Father in Heaven, You sit high
Way above the clouds in the sky
Also, You even look low
To see that we know the way to go.

Father in Heaven, Thank You for all
The love You showed when You called
Us to be Your children during the fall
Father in Heaven, You are OH SO TALL!

PART 2:
Encouragement
for
Your Soul

Wait On The Lord

Wait on the Lord and do not fret
He will fulfill your heart's desire
Be patient, he is not through with you yet
The Lord is the One to admire.

Wait on the Lord and do not be discouraged
Because the time is near
In the end you will be encouraged
And have nothing at all to fear.

Wait on the Lord, He will give you His best
Because He loves you so much
The Lord is the best above the rest
And His best is His loving touch.

Use Me, Lord

I want the Lord to use me
He knows my every need
He wants me to be the best I can be
Since He has planted the seed.

Before I knew what was best for me
I was searching all the day long
For I was blind and could not see
I was singing a lonely song.

Use me, Lord, to the glory of You
Use me, Lord, through and through
Use me especially when I am blue
Use me, Lord, to make me brand new.

Supreme

What does it take to be Supreme
And walk around with a beam?
Not only walk, but glide with a gleam –
As strange as it may seem.

To be the best that you can be
To reach the highest height
To be what all eyes can see
What you put forth with all your might.

What does it mean to be Supreme?
You do not need to be tall and lean
Just look to God and you will know
You can dream the impossible dream.

Promises

Promises are not merely dreams
But something to strive for that is true
To believe all you can as much as it seems
To make your life brand new.

A promise is something that comes
from up high
It is good and it is fair
Oh my, my, my, my
It is good, it is fair, also something
you can bear.

What is nice about promises is they are for real
Because God gives them from up above
His promises are always fully sealed
As these promises are guaranteed
with His Love.

The Christian Way

Why not try the Christian Way?
Do not put it off another day
You may regret when you begin to play
That you will turn and begin to stray.

The Christian Way is oh so nice
It keeps you on the straight and narrow
You will not find yourself cold as ice
Because your eye is on the sparrow.

So get on board the Christian train
You can do so in the rain
Stop your whining and do not complain
You have a great deal to gain.

To Be Christlike

What does it mean to be Christlike?
No, you do not go out and ride a bike
You do not need to take a hike
But you make a meaningful, positive strike.

Christlike is growing strong in the Lord
Using the Word as a mighty sword
Standing tall for what you believe
And knowing in the Lord you are received.

Being Christlike takes a special thing
And that is allowing the Lord to bring
What He wants so you can mount up
with wings
For He is your Lord and King of Kings.

Hang In There

Do not give up when things seem bad
Such things that make you sad
Sometimes they even make you mad
But listen to something that will
make you glad.

God loves you over all
He loves you when you fall
So hang in there and stand tall
For you are the one He will call.

Hang in there, for God's sake
Hang in there, He can make
You feel that you can awake
God makes you have what it takes.

Faith

You need faith to get by
You cannot believe by yourself
If you do or attempt to try
You might as well put it on the shelf.

Faith makes you go to the next step
You feel so good you go with some pep
It is great knowing when you have slept
That Someone sees that you are kept.

Faith is believing with all your heart
So do not stop once you start
Have faith in God and you will see
He loves you; that is how it will be.

Do Not Give In

I want to say "do not give in"
For if you do you will commit sin
And if you wish to believe in men
There is no way you can win.

Do not give in; God is the One to trust
Call on Him – please, you really must!
If you do not and start to lust
Your life before you begins to rust.

Do not give in; God is the only way
This is why I want to say
That you should know every day
In Christ is where you are to stay.

Dear Lord

Dear Lord, we need You today
We need You in a special way
Touch us so we can say
That we will not go astray.

Dear Lord, step in and take control
Do not leave us in the cold
We want our names on the roll
And we want to walk on the streets paved
with gold.

Dear Lord, keep me still
Dear Lord, make me feel
Worthy to use my skill
As it is Your Perfect Will.

Prayer

We need Prayer all the time
More than a nickel or a dime
Prayer will help and make you believe
That you can set out to achieve.

Prayer is sacred and sincere
So pray to God, my dear
He is promising and clear
So you have nothing to fear.

Prayer will lift you up high
Prayer will keep you by and by
You will not have to sigh
Prayer will take you to the sky.

Who Loves You?

You are looking for worldly love
That does not fit like a glove
When you are rejected, do not become unglued
Just ask yourself honestly, "Who loves you?"

We look for love in all the wrong places
Running to people wearing false faces
But we must look for the One who traces
Our lives completely and fills
the empty spaces.

So, you need to take your cue
Looking for love without a clue
Remember there is One who is true
This someone is God, who loves you!

The Brighter Side

Let me tell you how you can glide
You must be humble and not full of pride
So if you want to take this spiritual ride
You will find the Brighter Side.

You do not have to have fame
Do not be embarrassed or even ashamed
Because you are not the same
The Brighter Side is calling the Lord's name.

You cannot run, you cannot hide
Learn to listen and to abide
By Him, your Heavenly Guide
For Jesus is the Brighter Side.

Watching Over Me

When I think I am on my own
And danger makes me have such fear
I must realize I am not alone
For Someone is always near.

No matter where I am to go
I cannot run, I cannot hide
He searches for me to and fro
And lets me know He is on my side.

He is the One who set me free
My eyes are open, now I see
And now I know all the time it was He
Jesus Christ watching over me.

The Burden-Bearer

Life's problems will never go away
They take you to the end of your rope
Have faith, courage, and always pray
Because the Burden-Bearer gives you hope.

People take their problems everywhere
But to the One who really cares
Take your burdens to Him and
leave them there
For this is something He can bear.

Come to Him; He will lift the heavy load
He will even put you on the straight
and narrow road
You will find your life is no longer in error
For Jesus Christ is truly the Burden-Bearer.

Believe!

If you have difficulty trusting some things
Because of the outcome such may bring
Put your trust in Someone who is real
So you can wear the eternal seal.

When you think that all has failed
And you have nothing to look forward to
There is Someone who is on your trail
To see that your life becomes brand new.

So, do not wonder because you may grieve
And you may very well be deceived
Just have faith, be patient, and you will receive
God's Gift if you only BELIEVE!

Ordinary People

It is ordinary people like you and I
Who can have the pie in the sky
If we can firmly take a stand
And allow the Lord to lead us by His hand.

It is ordinary people who are lost
That God goes after at all cost
The persons who are out in the world
He makes their skin tingle and their hair curl.

Ordinary people learn to surface
With God; your life has a purpose
That you can fulfill in this time and space
For in eternity, you take your place.

I Am Satisfied

I am satisfied in my present state
Because of my life and my fate
God saved me before it was too late
So, I know that He is oh so great!

With our lives we should be content
For Jesus came then He sent
The Holy Ghost, who spent
Time with us since Jesus went.

I am satisfied with my life now
I am satisfied, I will tell you how
Jesus is my friend and pal
How I look to Him and bow.

What You Can Bear

God knows what you can bear
He knows your every want and need
He watches over you and shares
What you desire in thought and deed.

When you think times are hard
Trust in God and do not discard
The strength He gives on His regard
Because He makes easy what seems hard.

God knows what you can bear
You cannot turn your back, you do not dare
He lifts you up and wants to share
What He has for you because He cares.

He Is There

When you are in trouble and sad
And you feel that no one cares
Be still, listen; things are not bad
God hears you and He cares.

He is with you, call on Him
He is there when things seem dim
You learn to realize with a whim
With God your life is not slim.

He is there in the midst of the storm
He is there in great form
You can live according to His norm
In God's love, which is gentle and warm.

To The Sky

Keep your head to the sky
Go ahead, I will tell you why
God sees you by and by
You will be amazed at what is on high.

Look to the One who cares
Look to the One whose blood was shed
Jesus sacrificed His life to bear
Our sins so He could be raised from the dead.

Keep your head to the sky
He will see you through by and by
You know the reason and why
Jesus died and how He sits on high.

Brand-New Life

When you are tired of the way things are
And you are not getting too far
Pray that things will get better
A brand-new life is a real go-getter.

God makes you feel brand new
No matter what you are going through
He is the One you are to turn to
God is better than a dream come true.

So be prepared for anything
Of what God will surely bring
Do not let your heart fill with strife
God is giving you a brand-new life.

Forgive Us

We tend to live and do as we please
Caring for what we want and how
We make fun as well as tease
But we need to think hard right now.

Look to the Lord when we stumble
Speak up and do not mumble
Pray that we will not tumble
Ask for forgiveness and be so humble.

Forgive us, Lord, for we are wrong
We have been in sin much too long
Fill us with a precious song
Your forgiveness makes us strong.

You Are Never Alone

When you feel no one is around
And you are on your own
Sit quietly, listen to the sound
You will find you are never alone.

When you need someone for comfort
He will bless you and you can report
Knowing with your heart you can resort
To God because you will not come up short.

So if you are lonely, use the eternal phone
Call the Almighty One who sits on the throne
He will fill you up and set the tone
You will know that with God, you are
never alone.

Gentleness

Gentleness is something that we acquire
When the Lord comes into our lives
That is one of the fruits that require
That we live with determination and drive.

Gentleness is a calm side
It is something that we should not hide
For being on the Christian ride
We should not take this all in stride.

This is something we need to work on
Before time runs out and is gone
If we want and plan to be God's child
We need Gentleness and to be meek and mild.

The Road

The Road that we travel in life is long
We can become weary and weak
But in order to gain strength and
become strong
Pray to God for a winning streak.

The Road is narrow and it is straight
It gets better if you wait
You will know once you reach that gate
That God is on time and never late.

Yes, the Road is long, it is true
But here is what you have to do
Trust in God for what He makes long
For traveling this Road will make you strong.

Your Heart's Desire

When you want your heart's desire
You search around to and fro
You become lost and tend to get tired
And learn you have no place to go.

You need to look in only one place
To God up above with a humble face
To get your life in order with a pace
To run in God's glorious race.

So look around, but do not get tired
Do not worry about the fire
God is the One to truly admire
Because He gives you your heart's desire.

What You Need

There is One who knows what you need
He knows what is best for you
He will not let you get hungry with greed
But with Him life is sunny and new.

Pray for what God wants for you
Ask Him to help you accomplish and do
His will that is perfect, righteous, and true
To overcome obstacles you go through.

God knows what you need
He loves all and He feeds
Those who are not selfish with greed
But begin to grow when He plants the seed.

Be Content

"Be content," I would like to say
Be content not only today
Be satisfied with the here and now
Because God shows you the way and how.

That is all that is required of you
Here is what you have to do
Have faith and trust in God through
The troubles that will set you anew.

No, you do not have to rent it
Be patient, God sent it
Yes, He really meant it
That is why we are to be content.

In Times Of Trouble

In times of trouble you should know
You stand tall and go with the flow
Because God fills you with a glow
To live for Him as He tells you so.

In times of trouble you need a friend
One who will stand by you through
thick and thin
A Friend who starts or begins
To see you all the way to the end.

In times of trouble God hears your cry
He will change your life if you trust and try
He gives you more and never less
In Jesus Christ you are truly blessed.

To Be A Star

What does it take to be a star?
You do not have to look very far
You do not need to drive a fancy car
You will not get hurt nor get a scar.

A star does not have to be on stage
Or be someone loud in a rage
A star is someone who shines bright
When God touches them with His Light.

What does it take to be a star?
Now you can look near and not far
Forget about that fancy car
God made you the star that you are.

Give It Up

Give it up; what do you have to lose?
Your life will improve if you choose
To give it to God up above
For He will give you perfect love.

Give up your life, it will be alright
Give it up now before the night
Your life will be wonderful in God's sight
You will soar like an eagle high in flight.

Give it up before it's too late
Give it up, do not hesitate
To be what He wants you to be
God is the answer, He holds the key.

Call On Him

Call on Him when you are down and out
Call on Him for He will bring about
Peace and encouragement to help you stay
On the road you are traveling today.

When the strong winds arise
Then comes the heavy rain
Call on Him and be oh so wise
And believe you have everything to gain.

Call on Him on your account
Call on Him for you will amount
To the way He wants you to live
God wants you to have all He will give.

Trouble Don't Last Always

The hard times seem like a lot to bear
That is why you go through the days
Wondering if anyone really cares
But trouble don't last always.

There are some burdens that are on you
But listen to what you can do
Go to God, who will see you through
For God Almighty is oh so true.

The blessings will come if you hang in there
He answers you when you pray
God gives you all His love and care
So trouble don't last always.

The Precious Blood

When we search for peace and satisfaction
We tend to look in the wrong place
We get caught up in the attraction
Of how the crowd runs its race.

When you feel you are in doubt
Pray that God shows you a way out
Of carrying your burdens and sins about
You will feel much better, like you have clout.

The Precious Blood will cover your sins
It helps you to go on to the end
You will know you are on your way to win
The love of Christ as your new life begins.

What I Can Do

What I can do is not done alone
For my heart may be made of stone
I need Someone who sets the tone
He is the One who sits on the throne.

God fills me and gives me strength
To go on at any length
When I feel I am in my prime
God is with me all the time.

What happens to me fits like a glove
From One who is like a dove
He sends it from up above
What I can do is with God's love.

Your Touch

When I am weary, sad, and worn
I do not know where to turn and I feel torn
I search for You oh so much
For what I need is Your touch.

I need this when things are not right
I pray hard with all my might
For what is plain in my sight
Is that God touches me with His light.

Since this is what I need
In thought, word, and in deed
I will learn to take heed
To Your touch, which is the seed.

He Speaks

When things feel like a losing streak
You want to get up and take a peek
Plan to do so all during the week
God hears you and He speaks.

When He speaks you are to be still
Listen to Him and wait until
He tells you to move with a thrill
He speaks of what is His perfect will.

Now you have strength, you are not weak
Look long and diligently seek
His face when things seem bleak
God listens to you, then He speaks.

Which Way Do You Walk?

Are you known as a crowd pleaser
One who will toy and be a teaser?
My friend, before you start to talk
Let me ask, "Which way do you walk?"

You should know about the road you travel
Before it is too late and you begin to unravel
Turn to the Lord to show you the way
You know and believe He will
make a better day.

Before you get involved with the bulk
Of people who harm and like to stalk
Pray to the Lord, then let Him talk
Then ask yourself, "Which way do you walk?"

Shine On Me

Lord, it is wonderful to see
Your grace bringing me through to be
Who You have called me to be
Lord, I want You to shine on me.

When we are in the world, we are in the dark
So far away that we miss the mark
But when God steps in, we are like a lark
His light is what starts the spark.

The grace of God is what I see
The light of the Lord is here and will be
In my life, so I agree
Lord, I want You to shine on me.

Keep Your Eyes On Him

When we tend to look at madness
Which causes nothing but complete sadness
Before things start to seem dim
Try to keep your eyes on Him.

Jesus is Who we are to keep our eyes on
Before we become tired and also torn
For on the day He was born
It was our sins He has worn.

If you look around at what is dim
Things that seem bad and slim
Remember someone gives you a glim
Try to keep your eyes on Him.

God's Chosen One

(Dedicated to Apostle Charmaine Hollis)

God's chosen one, yes that is you
For His glory in you shines
through and through
This lets us know God is on your side
Jesus is your Lord, the Holy Ghost your guide.

A mighty work God has called you to
You may ask, "Lord, what do I do?"
Your life and your ministry are in His Hands
God chose you because He knew
you would stand.

Your beauty and your life He beholds
You are sure to come out as pure gold
For when it is all said and done
Apostle Hollis, You are God's chosen one!

You Cannot Hide

Let me say you cannot hide
No matter how hard you try
You should not take this all in stride
Or you will find yourself high and dry.

Whatever you do God knows about it
All and even the little bit
You better think before you get hit
And wind up in the bottomless pit.

Think long and hard about what you do
Because Someone is watching you
You will not get over or even slide
For with God, you cannot hide.

Heaven Smiles

What is greater than what earth has here?
It is wonderful, you have nothing to fear
You may even begin to shed a tear
When Heaven smiles, it is oh so dear.

When Heaven smiles, you can be glad
Because God forgives and He loves you
so much
You find that you were not had
As all is true and you can believe such.

Although we walk so many miles
We go alone and not in piles
Then we learn that it is on file
That God loves us and Heaven smiles.

Try Him

People do a lot of things for pleasure
Which could be called a crime
If they are looking for a treasure
Try Him – He is always on time.

When all fails and you do not know
where to go
You search long and hard, to and fro
There is one thing you ought to know
Try Him – He will teach and help you to grow.

He does not make life dim
Nor make your chances very slim
Your cup runs over the rim
God loves you – Try Him!

God's Unchanging Hand

Hold on tight, He will be here
Hang in there, you have nothing to fear
When you think you are on sinking sand
Hold on to God's Unchanging Hand.

He will not leave you high and dry
He will lift you up when you cry
You can be in His prayer band
Hold on to God's Unchanging Hand.

He makes you feel like you are grand
He makes you strong enough to stand
So that you may see the Promised Land
Hold on to God's Unchanging Hand.

Lord, My Desire Is To Be Closer to you!

There is no one I desire to know more
Because of what You say and do
For when You knocked, I opened the door
Lord, my desire is to be closer to You!

You searched for me high and low
You know what I am going through
Since I have no place to go
Lord, my desire is to be closer to You!

My life is now all brand new
It took some time, but You brought me to
Where You want me; this is true
Lord, my desire is to be closer to You!

He Open Doors

The problems of life can get you down
So much that a smile becomes a frown
But when you think you cannot
take it anymore
God blesses and He opens doors.

When you think there is no way out
And your troubles have you in doubt
Look around and all about
God's blessings will make you shout!

Just be patient; you will get more
Of what you need and what is in store
For you as God really adores
You because He opens doors.

Shower Of Blessings

You are unhappy because things are not right
You are discouraged and cannot see the light
He eases the suffering and the pain
What He has will take you to a higher plain.

Just hold onto His unchanging hand
Patience is the name of the game
What He has is extremely grand
You know that you are not the same.

The showers are known as the rain
But these showers bring no heartache and pain
Know for sure you can maintain
God's Showers of Blessings are what
you will gain.

Assured Acceptance

We like to know that we fit in
Even in crowds where we do not blend
But best believe you can win
With Assured Acceptance and One who
is a Friend.

You do not have to worry if you do not belong
He will change your life if it is wrong
You will sing His praises and even His songs
His Assured Acceptance will make you strong.

Do not worry if you walk alone
And search for answers that are unknown
His strength and power make Him call
you His own
God's Assured Acceptance comes
from His throne.

Do You Know Jesus?

Do you know Jesus, do you know Him at all?
Can you say He is the source of your being?
It is important that you listen to His call
Because believing is more than seeing.

Do you know Jesus, do you know Him at all?
When the going seems to get tough
Remember you do not have to fall
He will carry you when times are rough.

Do you know Jesus, do you know Him at all?
Get to know Him when you pray
Then you know you can stand tall
So, stay in His presence each day.

I Need You, Lord

I need You, Lord; take my heart
Fill me with Your everlasting love
Lord, take me and set me apart
And give me what You have above.

I need You Lord, You are the only Way.
Help me to love You more each day
I will listen to what You say
Because You will answer when I pray.

I need You, Lord; I know You are here
So I know I have nothing to fear
You opened my eyes and even my ears
I need You, Lord; You Are Very Dear!

Talk To God

We take our problems to everyone we know
Because we do not know where to go
Little do we know we do not have to go far
We can go to One who is a Shining Star.

We need to realize who He is
And spend more time with Him
Because we will learn we are His
And the problems are no longer dim.

We can talk all day long
Then we will learn where we went wrong
Go to Him in prayer and in song
Talk to God; He will make you strong.

He Lifted Me

I was once down in the dumps
And I saw no way out
I had some serious bruises and bumps
But with help I get about.

On my own I amount to nothing
I enjoy the love and care He brings
Jesus – yes, He is the King
And I feel I can mount up with wings.

I am truly on a natural high
Because of what He wants me to be
No way is this trip at all dry
For I know He lifted me.

He Saved Me

It does not take much to go wrong
Even when I want to do right
When I feel I will not last long
I try to win my own fight.

There are problems all around
Which seem to come my way
But I know I cannot be bound
For He hears me when I pray.

So when I feel at the end of my rope
The way is made clear to see
That God gives me the courage and hope
To know that He saved me.

No Turning Back

I have come such a long way
From the worldly track
For I listened and began to pray
So there is no turning back.

I know that Jesus is with me
When I cry out His Holy Name
I know some things I cannot see
But He is moving just the same.

He said He would be with me to the end
Because there is nothing I will lack
I know from all He will send
That there is No Turning Back!

Rest In You

The worries and troubles are all around
It will be that way I know
But there is courage that can be found
If I really know where to go.

You say, "Come and take your rest."
I say, "Lord, I cannot go it alone."
You say, "I love you. You are a part of My best.
I see you from My throne."

I will trust in You,
I have made You my choice
For no one else can see me through
I can live in peace and even rejoice
My Lord, I can rest in You.

No Room For Defeat

You cannot give up without a fight
Because you are not to be beat
So wear God's armor with all your might
For there is no room for defeat.

The devil will throw anything your way
That is why you should be steadfast
Call on Jesus for help when you pray
And He will make sure you last.

All of your battles can be fought for you
Yes, this is really a treat
God's love for you is so true
So, there is no room for defeat.

Jesus Supplies All My Needs

You have so much to offer me
If I only ask of You
Your perspective is better, I see
To make the old brand new.

I cannot look for help in all places
Because the answers are not there
What develop are empty spaces
But Lord, I believe You care.

Now I know I will look to the One
Who loves, nurtures, and feeds
I speak of the only begotten Son
Jesus supplies all my needs.

Everything Is Alright

I look around at the world today
For I want no part of it
I would rather stop and pray
So I know just where I fit.

You know, the world is pretty bad
But you need not be that way
You want to hear something to make you glad
Jesus comes into your life to stay.

Pray to get rid of fear and fright
So you can sleep in peace at night
The way to go is by His light
With Jesus, everything is alright.

I Must Go On

I must go on, I cannot look back
So I will leave the past behind
I want to be on the right track
And to live with peace of mind.

I must go on, there is more ahead
I cannot give up so fast
There is nothing to fear or even dread
For I know with Him I can last.

I must go on without a doubt
He said, "I hold the key."
There is no need to turn about
God's love dwells inside of me.

You Had Mercy On Me

As awful a life as I was living
There was good You could see
Your love is patient and giving
For You had mercy on me.

I ran from You for so long
Knowing full well that I was wrong
When I was weak, You made me strong
Now I praise Your name and sing Your song.

I desire to mature and to grow
And I want what you have me to be
Yes, I understand and truly know
Lord, You had mercy on me.

Victory

I will not claim defeat
Because my God is real
He is wonderful, oh so sweet
For He gave me the best deal.

I trust in Him to make a way
Regardless of my sorrow
I kneel and look to Him and pray
That He will bring me through tomorrow.

There is no way I can claim defeat
For my life is not the same
With God, who is loving and sweet
I have Victory in Jesus' Name.

The Master's Plan

The future holds more than you know
So forget about the things of man
Because of the way you should go
According to The Master's Plan.

The darkness may take over the light
You pray to God with all your might
Rest assured He will make it right
For you are beautiful in His sight.

He is working it out for you
Because you are for Him and not for man
He will lead you to what you must do
As part of The Master's Plan.

Because You Will Not Let Me Go

When I was on sinking sand
You really loved me so
I am now in the palm of Your Hand
Because You will not let me go.

When troubles seem to come my way
There is one thing I know
I come to You and surely pray
Because You will not let me go.

I love You, Lord, so very much
The joy I have will flow
Lord, it was only Your touch
Because You will not let me go.

Only For A While

The storms seem to rage all night long
You feel you are walking a mile
Keep praising Him and singing His song
The storm is only for a while.

Your blessings will come if you just hold on
To God's unchanging hand
He knew from the time you were born
That he would help you to stand.

God loves You, He will take care of you
You will no longer be sad and blue
Walk with God and you will wear a smile
Because trouble is only for a while.

Trust In God

Trust in God to see you through
No matter what others say to you
You find your way and what to do
His guidance will show you what is true.

Trust in God, He is right on time
Surely this is not a crime
He is certainly the Almighty One
Because it is His will that is done.

Trust in God, He is alright
Trust in God with all your might
Trust in God morning, noon, and night
Trust in God, then see the light.

Jesus Makes Me Glad

He makes me feel special and brand new
There is no need to be sad
He carries me through and through
Yes, Jesus makes me glad.

I wake up knowing He is with me
And I will go on to see what the future will be
Because of what my eyes cannot see
My faith holds me, for that is the key.

He Is the One who puts joy In my heart
He does not want me to be sad
I have to go on to do my part
Because Jesus makes me glad.

Faith Is The Only Way

I am not the same as I was before
This is so each and every day
I know I can go on more and more
Because faith is the only way.

Why would I hope if my eyes could see
What is right in front of me?
To be the best that I can be
As faith is the answer and the key.

What can I do, what can I say?
I go to God and humbly pray
He keeps me going so I will stay
Yes, faith is the only way.

Try Jesus

After you have tried everything
Give your life to Him
Then you will know what life will bring
As it is no longer dim.

Since the world is not for you
There is Someone who cares what you do
He is in your midst as you speak
Try Jesus because you are weak.

When nothing else will do
And you know you cannot cope
Look up and call on Him too
Try Jesus, He gives you hope.

I Can't Turn Around

I have given my life to Him
I was lost but now I am found
He lets me know that things are not slim
So, I can't turn around.

Now I can hold on and take stock
My foundation is the Solid Rock
My feet are planted on the ground
That is why I can't turn around.

God loves me, yes I know
I prayed and He told me so
He wants me to listen to His sound
God lets me know I can't turn around.

He Carries You Through

Problems surface, they start to mount
They are overwhelming, you feel down
for the count
When you are weak and weary, sad and blue
Rest assured: He carries you through.

Burdens seem heavy when they
come your way
You do not know how you will get
through the day
He will lift you up if you are still and stay
In His fold when you trust and pray.

Now you do not face your problems alone
He gives you peace and strength from
His throne
You will feel lifted, also quite new
With God's love and grace, he carries
you through.

Long-Suffering

Long-suffering is something all Christians
go through
Some do not like it at all
In order to make our lives brand new
Long-suffering helps us withstand any fall.

Long-suffering is not something one adores
Because it hurts and makes you sore
When you think you cannot take any more
God steps in and you go on for sure.

So expect long-suffering as a part of the test
Before you give up and prepare to rest
God is with you, He will give you zest
With long-suffering, you will know God knows you best.

Help Is On The Way

When you are in trouble with nowhere to turn
Help is on the way
Be of good comfort, good cheer, and learn
That God will help you today.

Do not give up without a fight
God hears you through your fear and fright
Help is on the way; do not turn out the light
God carries you through with all His might.

Be joyous, glad, and happy to say
God brought you to another day
So be still, quiet, and start to pray
In times of trouble, Help is on the way!

The Rock

When you feel you are sinking fast
Pray and stay in the flock
Do not fall or dwell on the past
Just stand tall on the Rock.

When you feel you are about to sink
You become thirsty and need a drink
You can get through with a wink
On the Rock you are stronger than you think.

Strive on, do not look at the clock
If you do you might get a block
Open the door when He comes and knocks
Jesus is the foundation and the Rock!

Strength

When you feel tired, down, and out
And do not know how to go about
Your daily routine at any length
Ask God to touch you and give you strength.

God's word will lift you when you are sad
It makes you encouraged as well as glad
There is no need to become extremely mad
You will achieve more than you ever had.

So when you think things look bleak
Be strong and do not become weak
Pray you will go to the greatest length
You are sure to succeed with God's strength.

Heaven-Bound

When you need a lift from the ground
Or a foundation which is sound
Change your life and turn around
In no time you will be Heaven-Bound.

Changing your life does not take much
Give up the things that are a crutch
His glory will give you such
A joy when you feel God's touch.

Now you are up, no longer down
You are not lost, but you are found
When you leave here you will get a crown
You are sure to be Heaven-Bound!

Here Is Something For Everyone

Do you need love, hope, and encouragement?
This is the book for you!
Receive God's love through His beautiful Art of Poetry
Praise & Encouragement

About The Author

Sandra M. Riley is a Born-Again Christian who is saved, sanctified, and filled with the Holy Ghost. She has made Jesus "the center of her joy." Sandra is a native of Chester, Pennsylvania. She received her Bachelor of Arts degree from Lincoln University in Pennsylvania, her Master of Social Work degree from the University of Pittsburgh, and her Doctorate degree in Higher Education from Walden University. Sandra is a member of God's House of Glory Haven of Peace in Chester. Through her God-given talent and the leading of the Holy Ghost, Sandra has written poems to praise God and to encourage the soul. Praise & Encouragement was written out of a desire to do something for God, giving Him all Glory, Honor, Praise, and to encourage souls that true happiness is in Jesus Christ. Enjoy reading God's Anointed Work Through Poetry. Be Blessed!

www.ingramcontent.com/pod-product-compliance
Lightning Source LLC
Chambersburg PA
CBHW060329130626
46553CB00003B/953